The Totally Out There Guide To GLACIER NATIONAL PARK

DONNA LOVE

ILLUSTRATED BY
JOYCE MIHRAN TURLEY

2011
Mountain Press Publishing Company
Missoula, Montana

Library of Congress Cataloging-in-Publication Data

Love, Donna, 1956
    The totally out there guide to Glacier National Park / Donna Love ; illustrated by Joyce Mihran Turley.
        p. cm.
    Includes bibliographical references and index.
    ISBN 978-0-87842-566-2 (pbk. : alk. paper)
    1. Glacier National Park (Mont.)—Description and travel. 2. Natural history—Montana—Glacier National
Park. 3. Glacier National Park (Mont.)—History. I. Title.
    F737.G5L68 2010
    917.86'52—dc22
            2010026253

PRINTED IN HONG KONG

MP Mountain Press
PUBLISHING COMPANY
P.O. Box 2399 • Missoula, MT 59806 • 406-728-1900
800-234-5308 • info@mtnpress.com
www.mountain-press.com

For my sisters, Diana, Darlene, and Delana, who first visited Glacier National Park with our parents and me in 1966 on a family vacation. Due to an August snowstorm we didn't make it to Hidden Lake on Logan Pass, but one of my strongest childhood memories is holding hands with my sisters as we scurried back down the trail through sleeting snow to the Logan Pass Visitor Center. —DL

For my children, Jeff, Kim, and Nate, who enhanced my enjoyment of every outdoor adventure, including a memorable weeklong camping trip at Glacier National Park in 1997. Now that they're grown and have left the nest, our three "Junior Rangers" continue to value spending time outdoors. They have acquired a lifelong appreciation of the natural world, whether they are commuting by bicycle, hiking backcountry trails, or skiing above tree line. —JMT

ACKNOWLEDGMENTS

I would like to thank Amy Vanderbilt, Public Affairs Officer for Glacier National Park, for her help with the manuscript, Megan Chaisson for her expert review, and Steve Gniadek, former wildlife biologist for Glacier National Park, for his helpful review. I would also like to thank Dr. Daniel B. Fagre of the USGS Science Center in Glacier National Park for his help in understanding the park's glaciers. In addition, I want to thank Kim Allen Scott, professor and archivist at Montana State University Library; Bill Hayden, Glacier National Park website designer; Deirdre Shaw, Glacier's museum curator and archivist; and the Mansfield Library at the University of Montana for help with photographs. I also want to thank the Glacier Institute for the many resources they provide on the park's history and natural history, both online and in their bookstores. Finally, and always, I would like to thank illustrator Joyce Turley for her most helpful diagrams and lovely illustrations, and Mountain Press editor Lynn Purl and the Mountain Press staff for bringing it all together. —DL

I would like to thank author Donna Love, who fully experiences every topic about which she writes. Her depth of knowledge always includes personal photos and carefully selected references to make the research phase of my illustration project that much easier. I also thank publisher John Rimel and editor Lynn Purl of Mountain Press for their continued interest in publishing nature and science books for children. Their books open the eyes of young readers to the natural world just waiting to be explored—outside their own homes, or across the country. —JMT

CONTENTS

Where can you find gleaming glaciers, majestic mountains, and wild animals that live at towering alpine heights? Glacier National Park!

What is Glacier National Park most famous for? That's right—glaciers! How many glaciers does it have? Although it used to have many more, it currently has twenty-five glaciers. It has so many glaciers that Native people called the area the "Shining Mountains" for all the snow and ice that cap its mountain peaks.

Glacier National Park is famous not just for glaciers but also for its colorful, ancient mountains. The rocks that make up these mountains began forming over 1 billion years ago. Just think of it! At a time when most of the earth was covered in water, the rocks that would become the tallest peaks in Glacier were just beginning to form. Millions of years later, these rocks were pushed upward and, presto! The mountains of Glacier National Park were created.

Once settlers and tourists began arriving in this region, it wasn't long before people wanted to make the area a national park. National parks have features that are so rare, special, or unique that people want to protect and preserve them, natural and unchanged, for the enjoyment of everyone. Some national parks have fantastic waterfalls, others have deep canyons, and some have amazing wildlife. Glacier National Park has all of these and more, including spectacular glaciers, mountains, and wildlife. In 1885 naturalist George Bird Grinnell made his first trip to the area and was so impressed by its splendor that he later wrote that it was the "Crown of the

—Donna Love

The National Park Service Logo is shaped like an arrowhead, reminding us of the historic people and events preserved at national park sites. The lake, mountains, trees, and buffalo represent the natural world that's protected in all the nation's parks.
—National Park Service

Glacier National Park is famous for the many animals that live there, such as this moose at Swiftcurrent Lake.

Glacier National Park in the northwest corner of Montana is so far north it borders Canada.

Continent." Considering how many other beautiful wild places there are in Canada and the United States that's pretty cool. Grinnell and others asked Congress to protect the beauty of the area forever, so in 1910 Glacier National Park became the tenth national park in the United States.

How big is Glacier National Park? It's big! At 40 miles wide and 50 miles long, Glacier National Park is the fifth largest national park in the continental United States. Inside its boundaries are just over 1 million acres of land. That's bigger than the state of Rhode Island. With over 700 miles of trails, Glacier is a place people love to go for hiking. If an experienced hiker trekked 10 miles a day, it would take that hiker about four days to go from western side of the park to the eastern side, and about five days to go from the park's northern end to its southern end.

But it would be a cold hike in the winter. Glacier National Park, which borders Canada, usually receives a total of about 400 inches of snow each winter. That's over 33 feet! It's so much snow that many of its roads and trails close in winter. Then hardy visitors strap on snowshoes or cross-country skis and enjoy this winter wonderland.

But no matter when you visit, you'll probably see lots of animals. What kind of animals will you see? You'll see the kinds of animals that love to live in the mountains. You might see mountain goats and bighorn sheep scaling alpine slopes, or moose and elk browsing mountain meadows. And if you're really lucky, you could even see a grizzly bear or wolf roving the forest. Would you like to travel to Glacier National Park to see its glaciers, mountains, and animals?

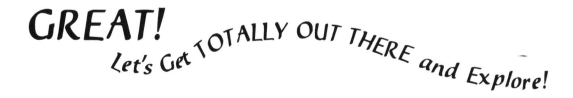

GREAT!
Let's Get TOTALLY OUT THERE and Explore!

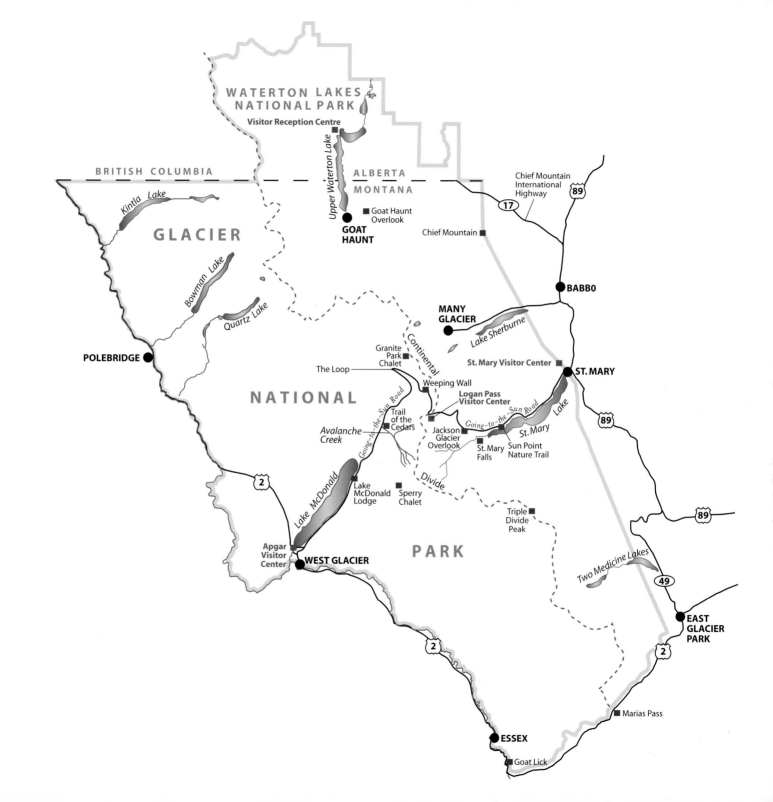

1

The Deep Freeze

Glaciers

As you already know, Glacier National Park is a land of glaciers. It has glaciers and it was shaped by glaciers, but just what is a glacier? It all starts with a single snowflake.

ICE SKATING
Snowflakes to Glaciers

When a snowflake falls to the ground and other snowflakes join it without melting, the snow builds up. When more snow falls than melts each year, the snow deepens and the weight of the upper layers presses air out of the lower layers, changing the white snow to blue ice. A large area of ice is called an ice field. When an ice field is about 60 feet thick it begins to move very slowly under the force of its own weight. When you have a moving ice field that remains from year to year without melting away each summer, you've got a glacier.

Can you move very slowly? Glaciers can. On flat land a glacier spreads in all directions, inching outward as its own weight presses one layer of ice over another. This movement

may be less than an inch a day. In mountainous areas like Glacier National Park, glaciers slide downhill. In summer a glacier in the park might slide 1 to 2 inches each day. That's pretty slow! At that rate it would take a week or more to move 1 foot.

SLIP AND SLIDE
The Park's Glaciers

Twenty-five glaciers currently lie scattered throughout Glacier National Park. Some have names given to them by Native peoples. Others are named after animals, early explorers, politicians, or park managers. Blackfoot Glacier, the park's largest glacier at about 400 acres in size, was named for the Blackfeet people, Natives who have lived near the park for centuries.

Hiking to see a glacier may be a lot more fun, but there are glaciers you can see without taking a hike, such as Jackson Glacier on the roadside at Jackson Glacier Overlook, and

◀ *Glacier National Park is home to twenty-five mountain glaciers, including Jackson Glacier, which is visible from Going-to-the-Sun Road. If you're really lucky you might see a golden eagle, too.*

Salamander Glacier above the hotel at Many Glacier. Seeing glaciers close-up is harder, but since you'd rather get totally out there, you'll be happy to know that it takes half a day or more of hiking to reach most of them. And while they're fun to see up close, they can be dangerous. The ice at the sides of a glacier moves more slowly than the center, so deep cracks known as crevasses often form. These may be hidden under snow, so even though you can hike to a glacier, you shouldn't go out on one—it's too dangerous.

MINI COLD SNAP
The Little Ice Age

When did the park's glaciers form? Scientists know that some ice was present in the park 7,000 years ago. They don't know for sure how long it was there or how often it melted. They do know that about 450 years ago the earth's climate cooled, starting a cold spell known as the Little Ice Age, which lasted about 350 years. Nobody knows for sure how the Little Ice Age started. It may have been caused by increased volcanic activity that blew so much ash into the air that less sunlight reached the earth. Or it may have been caused by a time of decreased solar activity, when less heat reached the earth from the sun. No matter what the cause, during the Little Ice Age the earth was a few degrees cooler than it is now, allowing more ice to build up on the mountains and turn into glaciers.

Sperry Glacier below Gunsight Mountain is one of the park's most famous glaciers. —Distress.bark/Wikimedia Commons

Glaciologists—scientists who study glaciers—know that at the end of the Little Ice Age there were about 150 mountain glaciers in the park. Today deep snow still accumulates, but summers are warmer and last longer, so most of those glaciers have melted altogether or shrunk so much that now they're only ice fields. The remaining twenty-five glaciers are smaller than they were just a few decades ago.

The U.S. Geological Survey, the federal agency responsible for scientific research in national parks, predicts that if the earth's current warming trend continues at the present rate, all of the park's glaciers will be gone by the year 2030 or sooner. Some will totally melt, and others will shrink down to ice fields that no longer move.

If all the glaciers melt, will the park still be called Glacier National Park? Yes! Most people assume the park was named for the mountain glaciers you can still see. However, many of the park's first explorers were geologists—scientists who study the earth. They were fascinated with the park's geology and the history of its mountains. The park's name has more to do with the Ice Age glaciers that carved the landscape than with the glaciers that remain, so the name will still fit even if the glaciers are gone.

FROZEN IN TIME
The Ice Age Glaciers

Starting about 1.8 million years ago, long before the Little Ice Age, huge continental glaciers—glaciers as big as continents—covered the park's mountains. These glaciers were so enormous they reached from the North Pole all the way through the northern United States and had an average depth of over 1 mile! Glacier Park's mountains aren't much taller than that, so only the tops of the tallest peaks stuck out above the glaciers like islands in a sea of ice. This Ice Age took place during a time known as the Pleistocene epoch. During the Ice Age the giant glaciers advanced and retreated at least four times. As the deep ice grew, flowed, and melted, it carved the mountains of Glacier National Park.

In the past, Iceberg Glacier, which is now an ice field, used to calf, or have huge chunks of ice break off, into Iceberg Lake. The resulting icebergs used to drift in the lake all summer. Nowadays any ice in the water is lake ice that freezes each winter and breaks apart each summer.
—© Fred Stillings/Dreamstime.com

Grinnell Glacier (center) *as it appeared in 1900, when it used to merge with Salamander Glacier* (above right). —F.E. Matthes Photo, courtesy of GNP Archives

This photo was taken in 2008 from the same spot, showing how much the glacier changed in a century. Grinnell Glacier has melted so much it can barely be seen from this vantage point. —Lisa McKeon, U.S. Geological Survey

MOUNTAIN MOVERS
Glaciers Carve Mountains

A glacier is very heavy. As it moves, the weight of the sliding ice plucks rocks out of the ground like a huge rock picker. The rocks get stuck in the ice and are then carried along by the glacier. A glacier can pick up large boulders as well as tiny pebbles, slowly sculpting the mountainside as it goes.

Depending on how deep the glacier is, and how many glaciers surround a mountain, many different mountain shapes can be created. When glacial ice surrounds a mountain peak on three or more sides, rocks are carried away from all sides, forming a pyramid-shaped mountain known as a horn. Two glaciers scraping against opposite sides of a mountain can form a long, thin ridge called an arête. The name comes from a French word that means "fishbone" since these long ridges look like the narrow, curving backbone of a fish. When the ice wears through an arête, a low place called a col or saddle is created. These are often places where people can pass over more easily than other places, so cols are often known as mountain passes. Logan Pass is a col with a road over it, making it the park's most-used mountain pass.

During the Pleistocene Ice Age, glaciers covered all but the tallest peaks in Glacier National Park, including here at Saint Mary Lake.

When a glacier slides downhill away from a mountain peak, slowly plucking rocks off the mountainside, it can create a bowl-shaped depression in the mountainside called a cirque. A mountaintop can also be worn down when warmer temperatures melt the ice at the top of a glacier, leaving a bergschrund, which is a gap between the mountain peak and the glacier. *Bergschrund* is a German word that means "mountain crevasse." Meltwater fills the gap and makes its way into cracks in the mountain. When the water refreezes, it expands and breaks off chunks of rock. This slowly undercuts the slope, leaving the mountaintop hanging over its base.

VALLEY ALLEY
Glaciers Create Spectacular Views

As a glacier flows downhill, it follows the path of winding valleys that rivers have already carved in the park's mountains. As the glaciers in the park slid down these channels or glacial troughs, the glaciers scraped rocks off both the valley floor and

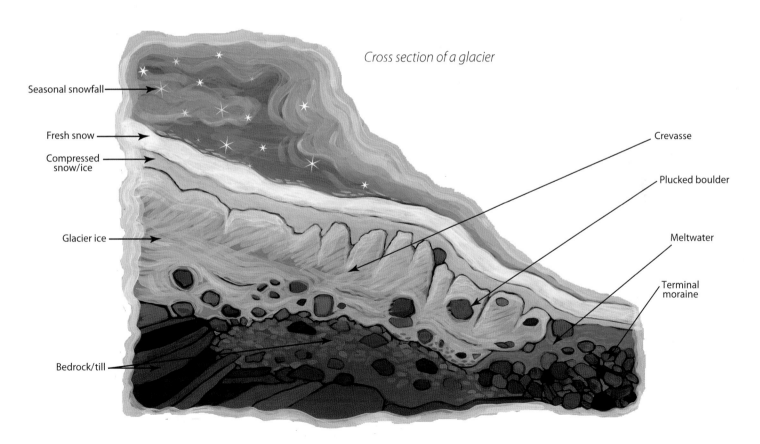

Cross section of a glacier

Seasonal snowfall

Fresh snow

Compressed snow/ice

Glacier ice

Bedrock/till

Crevasse

Plucked boulder

Meltwater

Terminal moraine

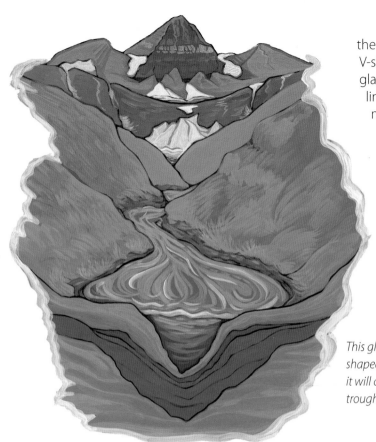

the sides of the mountains, turning the crooked, narrow, V-shaped river-carved valleys into straight, wide U-shaped glacier-carved valleys. Today, these valleys provide an open line of sight to the mountains, creating Glacier's sensational mountain views.

Along with the large U-shaped valleys, glaciers also created many hanging valleys. These small, glaciated depressions high on the mountainsides form when a small mountain glacier joins a deeper valley glacier. The smaller moun-tain glacier can scrape only a small valley out of the mountainside before joining a larger valley glacier. When the glaciers melt, the small mountain valley is left "hanging" on the mountainside.

This glacier has already created a U-shaped hanging valley. As it advances it will continue to carve a glacial trough in the existing river valley.

McDonald Valley below Logan Pass is a large U-shaped valley carved by glaciers.
—© Lawrence Stolte/Dreamstime.com

ROCK AND ROLL
Glaciers Move Rocks

Where did all the rocks go that the glaciers scooped up? When a glacier picks up a rock, it acts like a conveyor belt and slowly moves the rock along. The rocks carried by a glacier are known as glacial till. Till can be made up of everything from tiny particles of sand to huge boulders. When large amounts of till are dumped off at the edge of a glacier it can form a ridgelike mound known as a moraine. On the sides of a glacier this is called a lateral or side moraine. A terminal or end moraine forms when the till is dumped off the lower end of a glacier.

At the lower end of a glacier, water from melting ice can carry away some of the glacial till, creating outwash plains—broad areas that reach far beyond the glacier's end. Many communities around Glacier, such as Apgar and Saint Mary, sit on outwash plains of gravel left when the Ice Ages ended.

HEAT WAVE
The End of the Ice Ages

About 20,000 years ago, the earth's temperature began to warm and the Pleistocene glaciers began to melt, and they were mostly gone by 11,000 years ago. However, the Ice Age glaciers were so large and lasted so long that they created the wide variety of shapes found in the park's mountains today. When the colossal continental Ice Age glaciers melted, Glacier's wonderful new mountain landscape was revealed.

Lake McDonald is flanked by lateral moraines left by ancient Ice Age glaciers.

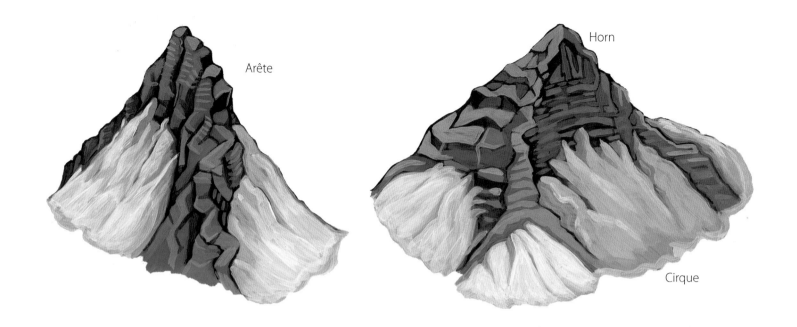

Arête

Horn

Cirque

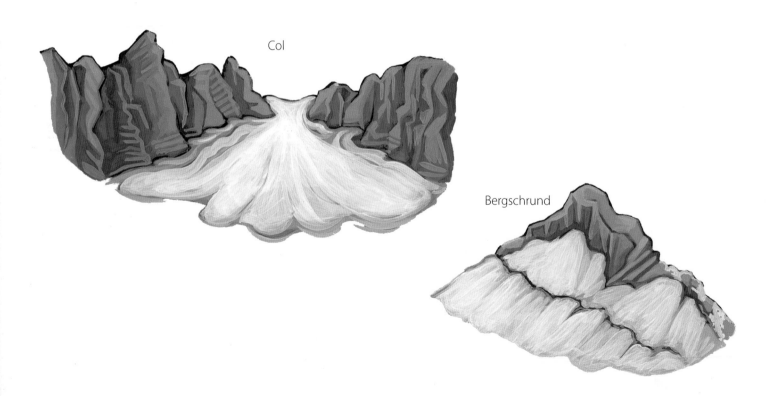

Col

Bergschrund

Mount Reynolds in the middle of the park is a glacier-carved mountain horn.
—Thomas Kriese, Wikimedia Commons

The 7-mile-long Garden Wall is a glacier-carved arête that runs through the middle of the park. —© JimParken/Dreamstime.com

Glacier National Park's mountains are famous for their glacier-carved shapes, but they are also famous for being made from some of the oldest, most well-preserved sedimentary rock on earth. Sedimentary rocks are rocks that form when sediments, such as sand, silt, mud, or organic matter from plants or animals, are deposited and harden to form solid rock. Ripple marks and mud cracks still visible in some of the rocks in the park reveal that most of them originally formed underwater. Then forces deep within the earth pushed the rocks skyward and giant mountain ranges were born.

FOUNDATION FORMATION
The Rock-Bottom Layers

Over 1 billion years ago a large body of water called the Belt Sea covered the area that became Glacier National Park. For over 800 million years, sediments settled on the seafloor and built up. Over the centuries, gravity and the weight of new layers compressed and hardened them into sedimentary rocks. The depth of the sea and the amount of minerals, especially iron, in its water varied over the years, so different layers have different colors.

The rock layers in Glacier are a lot like a layer cake. Each rock layer is known as a formation. The Altyn Formation is the bottom layer on the park's eastern side. This 1,400-foot-thick gray limestone layer was deposited when the water was warm and shallow. When this gray rock is exposed to air and water at the earth's surface, it changes to a tan color. The Altyn Formation can be seen underfoot at Many Glacier Hotel and along the Sun Point Nature Trail at Saint Mary Lake.

The Prichard Formation is the bottom rock layer on Glacier's western side. It formed at the same time as the Altyn and under the same sea, but it formed where the sea was deeper. Pressure and heat caused mud and silt to harden into a rock called argillite. You can see part of the dark gray Prichard Formation on Upper McDonald Creek at McDonald Falls, where the water pours over this 1.6-billion-year-old rock.

◀ *Mule deer graze below Chief Mountain, a mountain butte on the park's eastern side.*

Ripple marks on this rock in Glacier National Park show that it formed underwater.
—National Park Service

Mud cracks show that this rock formed at the edge of an ancient sea.
—National Park Service

The tan rocks in the foreground of this picture at Many Glacier Hotel are part of the Altyn Formation, the park's oldest rock layer.
—Traveler100/Wikimedia Commons

The Appekunny Formation was laid down on top of the Altyn and Prichard Formations. The Appekunny Formation is a 3,500-foot-thick green mudstone layer made from mud and silt that were deposited when the sea was deep and contained the mineral iron. The Appekunny Formation makes up the lower part of the park's mountains. It is now mostly covered in forest, but you can see this hard green rock scattered along the shoreline of Glacier's larger lakes and rivers.

The third rock layer, the Grinnell Formation, is a 2,500-foot-thick red mudstone layer. It also formed when iron was present in the water, but at a time the sea was shallow. This allowed the iron to oxidize, meaning it rusted in the air, giving the mud its red color. You can see the red rocks of the Grinnell Formation at Avalanche Gorge on the western side of the park and at Virginia Falls on the park's eastern side.

The fourth rock layer, the Empire Formation, is an 800-foot-thick grayish green mudstone layer. It formed at a time when the sea was in a state of change. It is a thin layer, so it isn't easily seen from a distance. You'll have a better chance of seeing it if you hike in the mountains. One good area to see it is at Many Glacier if you hike above tree line.

Virginia Falls pours over the red rock of the Grinnell Formation.
—© Lawrence Stolte/Dreamstime.com

The fifth major rock layer, the Helena Formation, is a 2,500-foot-thick light gray limestone layer, made when layers of algae built up on the seafloor when the sea was shallow. Rocks along the road over Logan Pass above the Loop and at Siyeh Bend are composed of the light gray rock of the Helena Formation. Much later, a vein of hot magma shot up through the rock layers and formed the Purcell Sill, a 100-foot-thick black rock stripe that streaks across the park's peaks high in the Helena Formation.

The Snowslip Formation is a 2,000-foot-thick layer that formed on sandy tidal flats. Its red and green mudstone rocks are sandwiched in brown sandstone. You can see it on Clements and Reynolds Mountains on Logan Pass. Sitting on top is the 600-foot-thick Shepard Formation, a golden brown limestone layer formed when the sea was drying out. Mount Cannon and Clements Mountain are good places to see the Shepard Formation.

Water cascades down the gray rock of the Helena Formation near the Loop on Going-to-the-Sun Road. —Donna Love

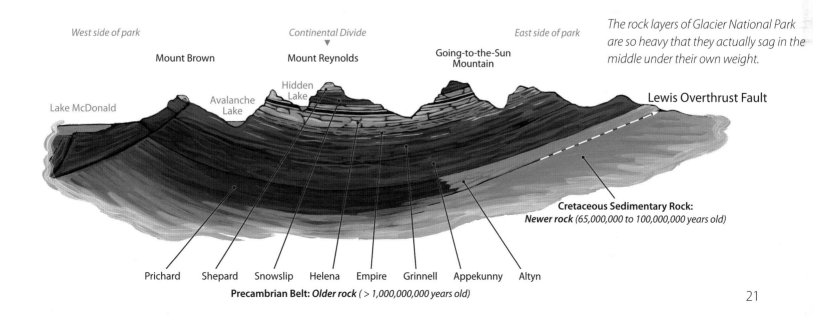

West side of park

Continental Divide

East side of park

The rock layers of Glacier National Park are so heavy that they actually sag in the middle under their own weight.

Mount Brown

Mount Reynolds

Going-to-the-Sun Mountain

Lake McDonald

Avalanche Lake

Hidden Lake

Lewis Overthrust Fault

Cretaceous Sedimentary Rock:
Newer rock (65,000,000 to 100,000,000 years old)

Prichard   Shepard   Snowslip   Helena   Empire   Grinnell   Appekunny   Altyn

Precambrian Belt: *Older rock (> 1,000,000,000 years old)*

MULTIPLY AND DIVIDE
Building Mountains

How did these underwater rock layers become tall mountains? Imagine grabbing a layer cake and pushing your hands together. Where would the layers go? Some would fold upward, some would break, and some would slide under the other layers. That's exactly what happened to the rock layers in Glacier National Park.

About 170 million years ago, Glacier's colorful rock layers began to slowly fold and rise, forced upward when the earth's tectonic plates—giant pieces of the earth's crust—collided with each other. The Pacific Plate, which lies under the Pacific Ocean, was pushing against the North American Plate, which lies under the North American continent. The pressure folded the rock layers upward and created the Rocky Mountains, a range that stretches 3,000 miles from Canada to New Mexico.

So many of the park's peaks slant upward in the same direction that early soldiers nicknamed them the "marching mountains," seen here at Saint Mary Lake. —Ken Thomas/Wikimedia Commons

The Rocky Mountains make up the majority of the North American Continental Divide, a line of connected ridges that runs from Canada to South America and determines the direction that water flows on the continent. On the eastern side of the Continental Divide water flows east toward the Atlantic Ocean. On the western side it flows west to the Pacific. Native people called the Continental Divide the Backbone of the World.

ROCK CLIMBING
The Lewis Overthrust

As the continental collision continued the rock layers kept folding. Then about 65 million years ago they snapped and a 300-mile-long section of the Rocky Mountains slowly slid upward and moved 40 to 50 miles east. As the section moved, an amazing thing happened. It didn't crumple like mountains often do. It rose in one giant slab and slowly rolled up

THE LEWIS OVERTHRUST

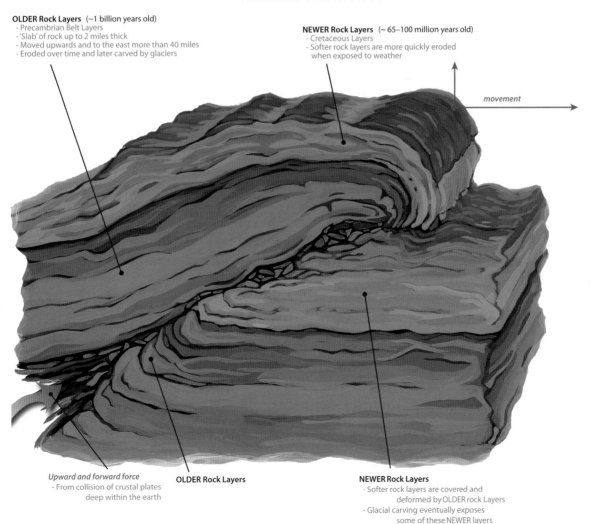

OLDER Rock Layers   (~1 billion years old)
- Precambrian Belt Layers
- 'Slab' of rock up to 2 miles thick
- Moved upwards and to the east more than 40 miles
- Eroded over time and later carved by glaciers

NEWER Rock Layers   (~ 65–100 million years old)
- Cretaceous Layers
- Softer rock layers are more quickly eroded when exposed to weather

movement

Upward and forward force
- From collision of crustal plates deep within the earth

OLDER Rock Layers

NEWER Rock Layers
- Softer rock layers are covered and deformed by OLDER rock Layers
- Glacial carving eventually exposes some of these NEWER layers

and over another formation, so you have an unusual case where older rock lies on top of younger rock. This type of giant rock movement is called an overthrust, and these particular rocks are known as the Lewis Overthrust.

One prominent eastern remnant of the Lewis Overthrust is Chief Mountain, a 9,080-foot-tall butte. It is made entirely of rock from the Altyn Formation, the oldest and sturdiest rock in the park. This rock is resistant to weathering, so when the huge continental glaciers, along with wind and water, carved away the surrounding rocks, the butte was left standing alone out in front of the other mountain peaks. —Photo courtesy National Park Service

COUNTIN' MOUNTAINS
Mountain Elevation

If you visit Glacier National Park, you'll see mountains so tall and beautiful you might think you're in the Swiss Alps. In fact, at one time Glacier's 175 mountain peaks were called the American Alps. However, Glacier's mountains aren't particularly tall. The tallest mountain in North America, Denali (in Alaska), is over 20,000 feet tall, while the tallest in Glacier is Mount Cleveland at 10,466 feet. Most of Glacier's peaks are between 8,000 and 10,000 feet in elevation, meaning how high above sea level they are at the highest point. However, they soar above the valley floors, so they look very tall. In fact, Mount Cleveland has the steepest vertical rise in the Northern Rocky Mountains. Its summit is over 1 mile higher than the valley below—that's over 5,280 feet!

At 10,466 feet high, Mount Cleveland is the tallest peak in Glacier. It also has the steepest vertical rise in the Northern Rocky Mountains, soaring over 1 mile above the valley floor below. —National Park Service

Glacier National Park is a land of weather extremes. In winter, some days are so cold it would make your teeth chatter. In summer, it can be sunny and warm, and even hot in the valleys, but snowstorms can also happen. In fall, mild golden days transform into frosty nights. In spring, the snow melts and the park's rivers and streams become rushing torrents of roaring water.

TODAY'S FORECAST
Temperatures and Precipitation in the Park

Like a three-car pileup, three conditions collide to create the park's weather: its elevation, its northern location, and the fact that it's fairly close to the Pacific Ocean. First, Glacier's elevation causes its weather to be pretty chilly overall. Even the lowest valley in the park is over 3,000 feet above sea level, so the average daytime temperature in summer is only 76 degrees Fahrenheit. On the mountaintops it is 10 to 15 degrees cooler. Even in summer nighttime temperatures may still drop below freezing. In winter the average daytime valley temperature is 21 degrees, but at night it can be much colder. The lowest recorded temperature was 55 degrees below zero, reported at Marias Pass in 1959. That's cold!

The second condition affecting the park's weather is the fact that the park is almost as far north as the Aleutian Islands in Alaska or Inner Mongolia in Asia. This northern position puts the park close to cold Arctic air. It also means that in the middle of winter Glacier receives only seven hours of daylight each day, so there's not much time for the sun to warm things up.

High on the mountaintops, weather stations like this one on the Garden Wall record temperatures and snowfall. —Mark Dundas, National Park Service

◀ *Above Saint Mary Lake a ptarmigan burrows under the winter snow, where it can keep warm while feeding on berries and seeds. These birds live year-round in Glacier.*

The Weeping Wall treats travelers on Logan Pass to a car wash—or a refreshing shower! —National Park Service

The third condition affecting the park's weather is the fact that the park lies only 550 miles west of the Pacific Ocean with no continuous major mountain ranges in between. This allows warm, wet ocean air, known as maritime air, to travel east to Glacier's mountains, where it encounters the cold, dry air that slips down from the Canadian Arctic. In winter, this mixing of wet weather from the west and cold from the north causes the park's spectacular snowfall of up to 400 inches each year, which is over 33 feet of snow.

Another interesting thing about Glacier is that its western valleys are greener, so it looks like they receive a lot more moisture than the eastern valleys, but actually both sides receive close to the same amount. The western side receives an average of 29 inches of precipitation, or moisture, a year and the eastern side receive 26 inches of precipitation a year on average. So, why does the eastern side of Glacier look so much drier? Warm, strong winds often sweep down from the mountain passes, so the eastern side dries out faster. Local people call these winds "snow eaters" for how quickly they melt snow on the eastern prairies. This wind is also called a chinook since it comes from the west where the Chinook people, as well as chinook salmon, live.

CAR WASH
Waterfalls in the Park

When the abundant snow in Glacier's high country melts in spring, it creates thousands of waterfalls. Many of these are nameless cascades that pour down the park's mountainsides. Others, like the Weeping Wall on the western side of the Garden Wall along Going-to-the-Sun Road, are among Glacier's most famous attractions. Glacial meltwater used to cascade down the mountainside, but after road construction blasted away part of the rock, water now seeps through the rock wall and falls on passing cars instead.

Running Eagle Falls on the eastern side of the park used to be called Trick Falls. When runoff is light, water flows only from the cave. In spring, when runoff is heavy, water also flows over the top of the falls.
—© David Ellingson/Dreamstime.com

GOT MILK?
Glacial Lakes and Churning Creeks

When a waterfall or stream flows into a mountain cirque, it often creates a small cirque lake, or tarn. Glacier has more than forty tarns, including Buffalo Woman, Morning Star, and Hidden Lakes. Some tarns are quite large. Iceberg Lake is 1 mile wide and 150 feet deep. Glaciers grind the rock they carry into powder called rock flour. The rock flour often gives smaller glacial lakes a distinctive milky green or creamy turquoise color.

Over 900 miles of icy streams fed by meltwater cascade through Glacier Park. Baring Creek tumbles 4,000 feet downhill in just 3 miles before emptying into Saint Mary Lake. That's an average drop of 3 inches for every foot it travels. Upper McDonald Creek, the longest stream in the park at 29 miles long, is so turbulent that it grinds the 1.6-billion-year-old hard, dark gray sedimentary rock of the Prichard Formation into rock flour that reflects sunlight, giving the stream its bluish green color.

Avalanche Creek swirls downhill so fast it created the crooked Avalanche Gorge. —Donna Love

STILL WATERS
Large Lakes

Like a waterslide emptying into a swimming pool, Glacier's swift streams slow as they reach the valleys below and spill into deep depressions carved out by the large continental Ice Age glaciers. Walled in by ancient lateral and terminal moraines left behind by the glaciers, these depressions fill with water to form several deep lakes.

Lake McDonald, the longest lake in Glacier, is 10 miles long and 472 feet deep. The second longest lake, Saint Mary Lake, is almost 10 miles long and 289 feet deep. Waterton Lake is 7 miles long and 500 feet deep, but only part of it is in Glacier Park. The larger, deeper part lies across the Canadian border in Waterton Lakes National Park.

Wild Goose Island in Upper Saint Mary Lake was named for a pair of Canada geese that nested there for years. Natives called this lake and Lower Saint Mary Lake the "Walled-In-Lakes." —Ken Thomas/Wikimedia

WATER FOR THREE OCEANS
Triple Divide Peak

Streams that drain Glacier's large lakes merge like traffic on a freeway to form several large rivers flowing away from the park. On the park's western side streams eventually join the Columbia River and drain to the Pacific Ocean. Streams on the park's southeastern side drain to the Gulf of Mexico and the Atlantic Ocean via the Mississippi River. Streams on the park's northwestern side drain to the Arctic Ocean through the Saskatchewan River and Hudson Bay in Canada. The remarkable Triple Divide Peak, a three-sided mountain horn in the Lewis Range along the Continental Divide, is the beginning point for three creeks. It is the only place in the United States where water from one mountain flows to three different oceans—the Pacific, Atlantic, and the Arctic.

Along with being an important water source for both the United States and Canada, the rivers and streams that flow out of Glacier are important pathways that allowed plant and animal species from all across North American to make their way to the park, contributing to the unique mix of wildlife that thrives there.

Water from Triple Divide Peak flows to the Pacific, Atlantic, and Arctic Oceans.

Northeast to
Hudson Bay

Southeast to
Gulf of Mexico &
Atlantic Ocean

West to
Pacific Ocean

4 Where the Wild Things Are

Forests, Wildflowers, and Animals

Glacier National Park is an ecosystem rich in biodiversity, where towering forests and tiny wildflowers grow. In the park's vast wilderness, animals of all shapes and sizes roam, from cute chipmunks to awesome grizzly bears. The variety of plants and animals makes the park one of the largest wildlife reserves in the United States.

FLAG FOREST
Forests of the Park

The park's unique location on the Continental Divide allows four distinct habitats of alpine, forest, meadow/grassland, and aquatic to lie close to each other. In this land of multiple habitats, alpine flowers meet prairie grasses and wet coastal-type forests live near dry, high-country woodlands.

In the mountains at about 6,000 feet, where it becomes too cold for most trees to survive, subalpine fir grows intermingled with whitebark pine in what is known as a krummholz forest. *Krummholz* is a German word that means "crooked wood," and it fits well. Here the trees are small and misshapen and often grow in miniature thickets. This protects the innermost trees from harsh mountain weather. Snow covers the ground for most of year at this elevation and the growing season is short, so trees in the krummholz forest grow slowly. At first glance the trees may look young because they aren't very big, but many are over 100 years old!

In the park's western valleys, west of the Continental Divide, some forests resemble a Pacific Coast rainforest of western red cedar, grand fir, and western hemlock. Pacific yew, a shrub mostly found on the West Coast, even grows in the park. Cottonwoods and paper birch, whose bark peels naturally as the tree grows, live along Lake McDonald. As the elevation rises, forests of Douglas-fir grow near stands of 150-foot-tall western larch. On the eastern side of the Continental Divide dryland forests of lodgepole pine, limber pine, and groves of aspen mix with grassy prairies.

◀ *Glacier National Park is home to many different animals, including grizzly bears.*

Trees of the krummholz can be seen at Logan Pass Visitor Center.
—© Lawrence Stolte/ Dreamstime.com

A great hike for kids on the western side of the park is the Trail of the Cedars, a handicapped-accessible trail through an old-growth forest of western red cedar.
—Donna Love

At high elevations, strong winds and blowing ice can break off the branches on the side of the tree that faces into the typical winds, causing the remaining branches to look like flags flying in the wind.
—National Park Service

FLOWER POWER
Wildflowers in the Park

In addition to forests, Glacier is home to over one thousand kinds of wild-flowers and other flowering plants, including shrubs such as mountain ash, dogwood, and serviceberry. In spring, wildflowers bloom in the valleys. In summer, alpine meadows on high mountain slopes burst with color. In the Hanging Gardens, a natural garden of rocks and plants at Logan Pass, just the right amount of warmth, dampness, and soil create small niches where growing conditions are favorable for wildflowers from all four of Glacier's habitats to grow near each other.

At high elevations the growing season is especially short. With so little time to grow, wildflowers have to make the most of the time they have. Glacier lilies, for example, sprout through the snow eager to start growing as soon as possible. Many wildflowers take up to ten years to mature before they blossom.

A favorite flower of the park is beargrass, a 4-foot-tall plant with a large cluster of tiny white flowers at its tip. In spite of its name, beargrass isn't a grass. It's a member of the lily family. And while some animals, including mountain goats, elk, and bighorn sheep, eat its leaves or flowers, bears don't.

Beargrass blooms every seven to ten years, so some years there are many blossoms and in others, not so many.

Camus —National Park Service

Indian paintbrush —National Park Service

WILD THINGS
Mammals

With its four main habitat types, Glacier can support a wide variety of animals. Fifty-seven kinds of mammals—fur-bearing animals that nurse their young—live in the park. Among members of the deer family alone this diversity can be seen with massive moose munching in marshy wetland meadows while great herds of elk stride across open grasslands and windswept prairies. Not too far away, mule deer delicately browse on twigs and branches, always listening for danger with their large, sensitive ears.

In summer, bull elk live apart from cow elk. In autumn, bulls join the herd for the rutting (mating) season. —National Park Service

Moose, like this bull wading in Waterton Lake, can be found in many of the park's wetlands. —© Hdsidesign/Dreamstime.com

Glacier has no fences. Animals roam freely, moving in and out of the park to surrounding areas. Grizzly bears and black bears are active from spring to fall, feeding on roots, berries, insects, and carrion—the carcasses of dead animals. Some animals, like mule deer, elk, and bighorn sheep, migrate, but they don't travel long distances. They just move from lower to higher elevations and back with the changing seasons. Mountain lions and gray wolves, which prey on deer and bighorn sheep, follow their seasonal migrations.

Huckleberries are a favorite treat for bears. —Donna Love

A black bear cub tests its climbing skills. —National Park Service

Spying a bighorn sheep on one of the park's mountainsides is a highlight of any trip to the park. Only the rams (males) have the large, curling horns; ewes (females) have slender, slightly curved horns.
—National Park Service

Mountain lions are sneaky predators that like to hide while they watch for their prey, so you probably won't see one.
—National Park Service

Wolves were once wiped out in most of the United States but a few have always roamed Glacier, traveling back and forth to Canada, although they did not live full time in the park. Today wolf numbers are growing, both in other parts of the country and in Glacier. The wolf's smaller cousin, the coyote, can also be found in many areas of the park hunting mice, rabbits, and voles.

Smaller animals living in the park include rodents like beavers, chipmunks, and ground squirrels. Elusive creatures like the pine marten and fisher, both cousins of the weasel, creep through the dark forest. Their long, pointed noses and sleek bodies are perfect for tracking down squirrels and eggs in bird nests.

CABIN FEVER
Alpine Animals

Like glaciers, some animals live year-round in the alpine zone—the area high on the mountains above the tree line, where summers are short and winters are long. Even in the extreme conditions of winter at these heights, many animals are active. Canada lynx chase snowshoe hares through deep snow. Wolverines, the largest member of the weasel family, live in mountain cirques, where they dig for ground squirrels and hoary marmots, which survive the alpine heights by sleeping the winter months away in rock caves beneath the snow.

Gray wolf

In winter the pika, a small relative of the rabbit with rounded ears, lives in burrows in rocks and feeds on grass clippings. It harvests these clippings in summer like a farmer harvests hay, spreading the grass on rocks to dry, then storing it away for winter. Each tiny 4-ounce pika (just ¼ pound!) stores as much as thirty pounds of dried grasses in its underground home to eat during winter.

Pikas are also known as rock rabbits. When they spot danger they give a sharp call to warn other pikas to dive for cover. —National Park Service

Hoary marmots, a type of large ground squirrel related to groundhogs, make their home in alpine meadows and rocky slopes. —National Park Service

BILLY GOATS GRUFF
The Park's Unofficial Symbol

Glacier's most famous mammal is the mountain goat. Well, it's called a goat, but it's really just a relative of goats. It lives year-round above tree line, where it feeds on clumps of grass and lichens. A mountain goat's narrow body is perfect for standing on slim ledges. The way its skeleton is arranged allows all four hooves to fit on a ledge as small as 6 by 2 inches! And the spongy footpads on the bottom of its hooves, which are similar to a dog's paw pads, help it grip slippery rocks. In winter a mountain goat's thick white outer coat of hollow hair worn over an undercoat of wool keeps it warm, but during storms it shelters in rock

A mountain goat nanny rests high on a rocky ledge with her kid. The mother will keep her baby close to protect it from golden eagles. —National Park Service

Mountain goat babies are called "kids." Sound familiar?
—© Jim Parkins/Dreamstime.com

crevices. In summer it sheds its outer coat but can still get overheated, so in warm weather you might see a mountain goat resting on a patch of snow or in the shade to stay cool.

Of all Glacier's large animals, you probably have the best chance of seeing a mountain goat. Good places to look are at Logan Pass, along the Highline Trail on the Garden Wall, and at Goat Lick near Marias Pass.

SKY HIGH
Birds in the Park

With over 260 kinds of birds, Glacier is a bird-watcher's paradise. As with other animals, the park's four main habitats promote this diverse range of species. In the park's meadows and grasslands, red-tailed hawks hunt mice and garter snakes while peregrine falcons feed on small birds. In the forest, 6-inch-tall northern saw-whet owls hunt pocket gophers and voles. High in the mountains, Clark's nutcrackers, members of the crow family, feed on whitebark pine nuts. Another high-elevation bird, the white-tailed ptarmigan, a bird the size of a chicken, lives at tree line year-round. This bird is brown in summer but turns white in winter for camouflage. To stay warm in winter, it fluffs out its feathers and burrows under the snow, where it feeds on berries and seeds.

Clark's nutcrackers live
at alpine heights eating
whitebark pine nuts.
—National Park Service

The yellow warbler lives in the park
in summer and raises its chicks on
a diet of insects that it catches in
flight. —National Park Service

The Harlequin duck was named for the male's brightly colored feather pattern, which resembles a harlequin clown costume. —National Park Service

A rare bird called the black swift nests behind waterfalls, safe from predators.

Many of Glacier's birds can be found around its aquatic habitat, water. Common loons live on lakes, feeding on fish and raising their young. In swift streams the small American dipper, or water ouzel, runs underwater looking for insects. Rare harlequin ducks also summer in fast-moving streams, where they feed on aquatic insects in the water and raise their ducklings. High overhead, bald eagles and ospreys soar, using their keen eyesight to search for fish.

DIVE AND THRIVE
Fish in the Park

Twenty-three species of fish live in Glacier's lakes and streams. The park's water is so cold that one park legend tells of a special kind of fish that grows fur to stay warm. Of course that isn't true, but it is true that the only fish that live in the park are those that thrive in cold water. Trout such as westslope cutthroat trout are native, meaning they naturally occur in the park. Rare native bull trout are in danger of dying out, so they are on the Threatened and Endangered Species List, which is a list of plants and animals that may become extinct throughout all or a significant part of their range. Some fish, like lake trout and grayling, were introduced, meaning people originally put them there. Unfortunately, these nonnative fish can threaten the survival of native fish. Luckily the park still has clean, clear lakes and streams where native fish can thrive.

Spawning bull trout. —U.S. Geological Survey

5 Mountain Time
The First Humans in the Park

Artifacts, or human-made objects from earlier times, show that people began traveling through what is now Glacier National Park more than 11,000 years ago, and people have been going there ever since.

ON SACRED GROUND
The First People

The first people to travel through Glacier may have been the ancestors of modern-day Native peoples. These first people were hunters who didn't live in the mountains year-round. It was too cold, and the snow was too deep. They traveled to the mountains in summer to hunt wood buffalo and woodland caribou, two species that used to live in the park.

About 8,000 years ago, Native peoples began regularly traveling the Old North Trail, a route along the eastern edge of the Rocky Mountains that extended from Canada to Mexico. Some of these people settled near Glacier's mountains.

The Ktunaxa, which in English means "the People," settled around the region of the park. In the United States, they are known as the Kootenai. In Canada they are still known as the Ktunaxa. The northern Pend d'Oreille people, also known as the Kalispel, lived west of Glacier in northern Montana and Idaho. The Salish people, also called the Flatheads, lived southwest of the park. All three groups led a semi-nomadic lifestyle, hunting and fishing in the park's mountains, picking berries and medicinal plants, and gathering beargrass leaves to weave baskets.

On the park's eastern side, the Niitsitapi, which in English means "Original People," settled along the eastern side of the Rocky Mountains from Canada to Wyoming, including east of today's park boundary. They consisted of three groups: the Siksika, which means "black foot," referring to the dark-colored moccasins they wore; the Kainai, which means "blood"; and the Piikani or Piegan, which means "spotted robe." The U.S. government collectively called them the Blackfeet, so that became their official name in the United States. In Canada they are known as the Blackfoot. The Blackfeet hunted buffalo on the plains east of the park. They also traveled into Glacier's mountains to hunt and fish, and to harvest whitebark pine nuts, drying and storing them for later use.

The Blackfeet led a traditional lifestyle based on nomadic buffalo hunting east of the park.

Two Salish women on horseback in full ceremonial dress. Probably Mission Valley (south of Glacier Park), Montana. —Morton J. Elrod Collection, Mss 486, Archives and Special Collections, Mansfield Library, The University of Montana, Missoula

A Blackfeet woman mounted on a horse, dragging a travois behind her. She is carrying a fully beaded baby carrier on her back. —Missoula County History Series, Archives and Special Collections, Mansfield Library, The University of Montana, Missoula

Food and other resources were plentiful and relations between tribes were generally peaceful before the arrival of Europeans, but the introduction of guns, horses, new illnesses, and the near-extinction of the bison brought changes that caused some tribes to compete with each other. As more non-Natives settled near Glacier, Native peoples were eventually forced onto reservations. The Salish, Kootenai, and Pend d'Oreille were placed on the Flathead Reservation southwest of Glacier. The Blackfeet were placed on the Blackfeet Reservation east of Glacier. The Glacier National Park region continues to have vital spiritual importance for all of these groups.

CROWNS OF THE CONTINENT
Fur Trappers and Traders

Over 300 years ago, fur trappers seeking beaver pelts became the first Europeans to claim the park's land for their countries. At that time, beaver felt hats, made from beaver fur, were in fashion in Europe. To find furs, trappers followed rivers such as the Mississippi, Saskatchewan, and Columbia Rivers. The earliest trappers never saw Glacier's mountains, but they claimed the park's land by claiming a watershed—an area of land drained by a particular river or stream—for their king. Eventually different parts of the area were claimed by England, Spain, Russia, and France.

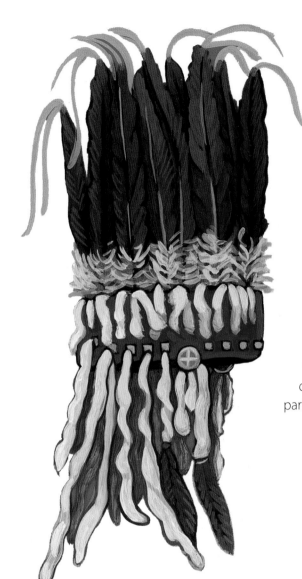

Some Blackfeet chiefs wore elaborate headdresses with feathers that stuck straight up.

Beaver felt hat

51

Blackfeet hunted American bison that roamed the Great Plains east of the park.

CONVICTION EXPEDITION
The First European Explorers

No one knows for sure who the first people of European descent to see the park's mountains were, but it may have been French Canadian brothers Pierre and François de La Vérendrye, who explored the area in 1742 and 1743. The first European to officially explore Glacier may have been Englishman Peter Fidler, a surveyor with the Hudson's Bay Company. Fidler journeyed to Glacier in 1792 and mapped the park's eastern side for the fur trading business, labeling Chief Mountain "King Mountain."

BORDER DISORDER
The Park's Northern Boundary

By the early 1800s, mountain men were making their way to the park's mountains. Hugh Monroe, a Canadian fur trapper, is thought to be the first person of European descent to actually live within Glacier's boundaries. He earned the trust of the Blackfeet and may have lived with them on the shores of Saint Mary Lake as early as 1832.

As more fur trappers and traders moved west, the United States and England both claimed the vast area of the Pacific Northwest that stretched from Alaska to California and east to the Continental Divide. The fierce debate was resolved in 1846, with land north of the 49th parallel going to England (later Canada) and land south of the 49th parallel going to the United States.

Heaven's Peak. When British trapper David Thompson saw the park's mountains in the late 1700s he wrote that "immense masses of snow appeared about the clouds and form(ed) an impassable barrier even to the Eagle." —Donna Love

The border between the United States and Canada today is marked with a wide, straight swath cut through the trees, visible at the far right in this photo, so hikers always know if they cross the border. —Acp, Wikimedia Commons

The U.S.–Canadian border at the eastern shore of Waterton Lake. —Traveler100, Wikimedia Commons

MOUNTAIN LORE AND ORE
The Park's Eastern Boundary

Around the time the Little Ice Age ended in the mid-1800s, fashions changed and the beaver fur trade died out. About this same time, copper and gold were discovered in Montana. Many people thought there might be ore deposits and oil in Glacier, so during the last half of the 1800s, as many as 15,000 miners converged on the area. Due to this, in 1895 the U.S. government pressured the Blackfeet into selling some of Glacier's eastern mountains back to the United States—lands that were originally a part of their reservation. Respected Piegan Blackfeet Chief White Calf told the U.S. government, "The mountains have been my last refuge. We have been driven here and now we are settled. From Birch Creek to the [previous] boundary is what I now give you. . . . We don't want our Great Father [the U.S. government] to ask for anything more."

In the end, only small amounts of gold, copper, and oil were found, so mining lasted only a few years. Ten years later, when the park was created, the western border of the Blackfeet Reservation became Glacier National Park's eastern boundary.

POLE BRIDGE
The Park's Western Boundary

When the Lewis Overthrust Fault formed about 65 million years ago, it pulled away from the rest of the Rocky Mountains to the west, leaving gashes in the landscape behind it. One particularly long, wide gash on the park's western side created the North Fork Valley. This valley is named for the North Fork of the Flathead River that flows south from Canada through the valley.

Native peoples used trails through the North Fork Valley to travel to hunting and fishing sites. When

Jay Polite Laber, an artist and tribal member who teaches at Salish Kootenai College, used found objects to create a series of horsemen sculptures titled "Sentries." They stand at each of the four corners of the reservation, welcoming people to the Blackfeet Reservation. —Donna Love

fur traders discovered the valley in the 1700s, they used it as a route to and from Canada. About halfway along the river on the American side of the border, a small trading post was built at the site of a log bridge. The tiny community became known as Polebridge. When the park was formed the North Fork of the Flathead River became the park's western boundary, leaving the western side of the river valley outside the park.

THE LAST PASS
The Park's Southern Boundary

Glacier's southern boundary follows Marias Pass and the path of the Great Northern Railway, built in 1891. At only 5,213 feet high, Marias Pass is the lowest pass in the Northern Rocky Mountains and an easy one for people to travel. Yet it was "lost" to explorers for nearly 100 years. If it had been found sooner, westward expansion of the United States

The Blackfeet were excellent horsemen, skillfully guarding mountain passes. —James Willard Schultz Papers, Collection 10, Merrill G. Burlingame Special Collections, Montana State University Libraries, Bozeman

might have taken this northern route to the Pacific Coast, and Europeans may have settled in Glacier's mountains sooner. That would have changed the land forever, and might even have kept it from becoming a national park.

For a long time only Natives knew exactly where the pass was. In 1804, one year after the Louisiana Purchase, in which the United States bought land from France that stretched from Louisiana to Montana, the Lewis and Clark Expedition was sent west to find out how much land the United States had obtained. While crossing Montana they came to a stream that flowed east out of the park's mountains and named it Maria's River, possibly for Lewis's cousin Maria. Later the river became known as the Marias River. On their return trip from the Pacific Ocean in 1806, the expedition tried to find its headwaters. If they had succeeded they would have found Marias Pass. The Blackfeet vigilantly guarded the pass, so other Native guides led fur trappers over different passes, and the location of Marias Pass remained a mystery to outsiders for decades.

In 1889, John F. Stevens finally surveyed Marias Pass and the Great Northern Railway built a railroad over the pass in 1891. Later, when the park was created, the 60-mile stretch of railroad over Marias Pass became Glacier's southern boundary.

After crossing Marias Pass, westbound trains follow the Middle Fork of the Flathead River to West Glacier.

PARKS AND RECREATION

Early Settlers and Tourism

When the Great Northern Railway was completed the company promoted the area's scenic beauty and wildlife viewing opportunities to encourage train travel. Railroad work camps in the area became towns, including East Glacier Park (originally Midvale), Essex, and West Glacier (originally Belton). Soon early settlers were making a living driving stagecoaches or ferrying visitors across rivers. Milo Apgar and his family rented cabins and provided meals at the end of Lake McDonald, so the little settlement there became known as Apgar. People who had grown up in the mountains—the children of fur trappers and mountain men—worked as guides, leading naturalists and scientists on expeditions through the area.

In the early days of the park, many people stayed at the Snyder Hotel on the banks of Lake McDonald. —Glacier National Park Archives

PARK IT
How Glacier Became a National Park, 1910

Before Glacier officially became a national park, the area was managed as a national forest. This meant that logging, mining, hunting, and cattle grazing could all take place, and many people thought Glacier needed more protection.

In 1885, James Willard Schultz, a mountain man who lived with the Blackfeet, submitted an article about the Saint Mary Lake area to the magazine *Forest and Stream*. The article inspired George Bird Grinnell, editor of the magazine and founder of the Audubon Society, to travel to the area. After seeing the region, he called Glacier's mountains "the Crown of the Continent," which remains one of the park's most famous nicknames. Over the next few years Grinnell urged the U.S. government to protect the area as a national park.

In 1901 Grinnell wrote, "No words can describe the grandeur and majesty of these mountains, and even photographs seem hopelessly to dwarf and belittle the most impressive peaks." Grinnell is sometimes called the Father of Glacier National Park, and several features in the park bear his name. Glacier National Park was established on May 11, 1910, becoming the nation's tenth national park.

It's not hard to see why Glacier is still known as "the Crown of the Continent."
—National Park Service

6 Road Mode
The Park's First Fifty Years, 1910–1960

Glacier National Park covers a lot of ground. The park boundary stretches 205 miles and includes more than 1 million acres. This huge chunk of land didn't have many roads or buildings when the park was created, so the early years were a time of building.

ROUGH RANGERS
The First Years

The first superintendent of Glacier National Park was William Logan, for whom Logan Pass is named. In the beginning, just six rangers patrolled the park. It was a tough job. One early park ranger froze to death while traveling between ranger cabins. Another was trapped in an avalanche for twenty-four hours but survived. Another broke his hip in a horseback riding accident and had to crawl for two days to reach help.

In spite of the dangers, a lot happened during the park's first ten years. Ranger cabins were constructed and trails were upgraded to gravel roads. An old trail to an abandoned oil well at Kintla Lake was upgraded to a gravel road known as the Inside North Fork Road. The park's headquarters, first located in a cabin on the western side of Lake McDonald, were moved to a building closer to the busy train station near West Glacier, where they remain today. Six years after Glacier National Park was established, the National Park Service was created in 1916 to manage the growing number of national parks in the United States.

In 1909, brothers John and Oliver Lewis constructed the sixty-five-room Lake McDonald Lodge using local stone and red cedar. Visitors arrived at the lodge by boat in those days, so it faces the lake. Today, when visitors pull up to the lodge by car, they actually arrive at the back of the lodge.

The first year Glacier National Park was created, four thousand people visited the park. In 1914 the Great Northern Railway started running buses from the railway stations to the park. The first buses had canvas tops that could open so visitors could enjoy the views of the park's mountains. Later, when a new fleet of buses was made for some of the nation's parks in the 1930s, Glacier National Park chose to have them painted red. Glacier's buses have been modernized, but the ones you can ride today are still those same red buses.

◀ *The famous red buses have traveled Glacier's roads since the 1930s. Drivers often had to jam the bus into gear while climbing a steep mountain pass, so the buses were nicknamed jammers.*

The first park rangers were hardworking mountain men.
—Glacier National Park Archives

Lake McDonald Lodge was designed to look like a Swiss chalet with steep roofs, shuttered windows, and multiple balconies. —Donna Love

The Great Northern Railway purchased land from the Blackfeet and constructed a 33-mile road east of the park with spur roads connecting to the new lodges they built on several lakes in the park. They also built trails and camps throughout the park, including nine small Swiss-style chalets a day's ride apart, so a visitor could journey through the park on horseback, staying at a different chalet each night. Most of these chalets and lodges are gone now, but visitors can still stay at the historic Glacier Park Lodge near East Glacier and the Many Glacier Hotel on the shore of Swiftcurrent Lake, as well as Sperry and Granite Park Chalets.

Horseback tours of the park were very popular, like this trail ride at Upper Two Medicine Lake. Horses are still allowed on many trails today. —H. T. Cowling, date unknown, James Willard Schultz Papers, Collection 10, Merrill G. Burlingame Special Collections, Montana State University Libraries, Bozeman

Park visitors can hike in for a stay at two of the historic Great Northern Railway chalets: Granite Park Chalet near Logan Pass and Sperry Chalet, pictured here, where you can also ride horses in from Lake McDonald. —National Park Service

IMPOSSIBLE DREAM
Construction of a Road Over Logan Pass Begins

In the 1920s, with so many tourist facilities in place, park visitation exploded to over twenty-two thousand people a year. So many travelers were riding the Great Northern Railway to the park that in 1921 the railway added a mountain goat to its logo to represent the park and its mountains.

By 1924 over thirty-three thousand people were visiting the park each year. Between 1925 and 1931, Eagle Scouts with the Boy Scouts of America made a big contribution to the park by building trails each summer. Many visitors still arrived by train, but car travel was increasing, too, so pressure to build a road through the middle of Glacier for visitors and park staff was growing.

Thousands of years ago, two Ice Age glaciers scoured a low place in the mountains at Logan Pass. At 6,646 feet, it's one of the lowest passes within the park boundary, but it's steep. To cross Logan Pass, people used to climb a series of steep, narrow switchbacks on foot or horseback. On the western side, there was already a road to Avalanche Creek that ended at a campground. On the eastern side there was a road along the north shore of Saint Mary Lake nearly to Sun Point. So in 1924, a route was surveyed over Logan Pass to connect the two points.

The way mountain roads are usually built it would have taken fifteen hairpin turns, or switchbacks, for a vehicle to climb out of the steep McDonald Valley, and three to descend down the other side to Saint Mary Lake. The hairpin curves would have been visible from miles away, detracting

In keeping with an old Swiss custom, locomotive bells, like this one on Piegan Pass, were placed on five mountain passes for hikers to ring, signaling to friends below that they had safely reached the pass.
—Glacier National Park Archives

Early travelers on Logan Pass didn't let a little snow stop them from enjoying the ride. —Glacier National Park Archives

from the surrounding scenery, so a young landscape architect named Thomas Vint proposed a longer route that would use only one switchback on the western side of the pass. Park management agreed, so the longer route was used.

In 1925 construction began on the road's western side. It took five summers to reach the top of the pass. At the height of construction, three hundred men, sixty mules, and ten horses worked on the road daily. In 1929, the gravel road to the top of Logan Pass from the west opened to vehicles. That first year, nearly fourteen thousand cars traveled the road from Lake McDonald to the top of Logan Pass and back again.

Retaining walls over Logan Pass, like these at Triple Arches, were built of local rock to blend in with the landscape. Construction in places like this was very dangerous. —Glacier National Park Archives

FRIENDS FOREVER
Waterton-Glacier International Peace Park

Before 1930 no road connected park headquarters near West Glacier to the park's eastern side. If park employees wanted to get from one side of Glacier to the other, they had to take a train. It would have been fun, but not very efficient. If there was an emergency, they had to wait for the train, so it was also important to complete a highway over Marias Pass. When the 57-mile-long section of U.S. Highway 2 was completed in 1930, it was the first road to connect Glacier's eastern side to its western side.

Waterton Lakes National Park in Canada, established in 1895, lies just north of Glacier National Park. When Highway 2 was completed, travel became easier between the two parks. In 1931 Rotary International service clubs in Montana and neighboring Alberta, Canada, suggested making Waterton Lakes National Park and Glacier National Park an international peace park to celebrate the peaceful border between the United States and Canada. The U.S. and Canadian governments agreed, and Waterton-Glacier International Peace Park, the world's first peace park, was founded in 1932.

PASS IT ON
Going-to-the-Sun Road Opens

Construction crews sometimes worked around the clock in twelve-hour shifts for two summers, finally completing the road over Logan Pass in 1932. But the road didn't have a name. The Blackfeet called one of the big mountains on the eastern side of Logan Pass "To-the-Sun-He-Goes Mountain." This referred to their belief that Napi, the son of the Sun and the Moon, came down to earth to help the Blackfeet. When he returned to his home in the sky, they believed he traveled by way of the mountain.

In the 1880s, James Willard Schultz, a mountain man who had lived with the Blackfeet, called the mountain Going-to-the-Sun Mountain. Park naturalist George Ruhle and Montana congressman Louis Cramton are both credited with suggesting Going-to-the-Sun Road as the new road's name.

Four thousand people attended the dedication ceremony in 1933. Many of them were also there to celebrate the new Waterton-Glacier International Peace Park. At the close of the road's dedication, members of the Blackfeet, Salish, Kootenai, and Pend d'Oreille gathered in a moving ceremony to share the pipe of peace, commemorating lasting peace between all people.

Going-to-the-Sun Mountain provided a spectacular backdrop as crews worked to complete the road over Logan Pass. —National Park Service Archives

NO PARKING
The Great Depression and World War II

With the completion of the roads over Logan and Marias Passes and the dedication of the International Peace Park, the park's future looked bright. However, not long before, in 1929, the Great Depression had begun. With millions of people out of work and many losing their homes, park visitation plummeted. At the same time, surprisingly, construction in the park actually increased.

To provide work for the nation's unemployed men, the Civilian Conservation Corps (CCC) was established, and men from across the country were put to work in national forests and parks around the nation. Between 1933 and 1942, up to fourteen CCC camps with 50 to 250 men worked in Glacier National Park fighting forest fires, clearing hazardous trees, putting in a telephone cable to the top of Logan Pass, clearing garbage, preparing campground sites, and installing water and sewer systems throughout the park.

In 1942, due to U.S. entry into World War II, the CCC camps shut down. With people and money devoted to the war effort park visitation dropped even more. Instead of tourists the Great Northern Railway began transporting troops and army supplies over Marias Pass. The five locomotive bells on Glacier's mountain passes were removed and used as scrap metal for the war effort.

VACATION NATION
The Park Rebounds

In 1945, when World War II ended and prosperity slowly returned to the United States, people started traveling to Glacier again. In 1946, over two hundred thousand people visited Glacier. In the 1950s car production surged and new highways crisscrossed the nation. It was a joyous time for many people. The war was over, jobs were plentiful, and people could afford the new cars and a family vacation to go along with it. During the 1950s over half a million visitors traveled to Glacier each year.

Car travel was becoming so popular that trains had a hard time competing. In 1955, the Great Northern Railway introduced its fast Orient Express streamliners to try to attract passengers. But passenger numbers continued to decline and by 1970 many railroad companies closed or merged with other companies. In the late 1970s Amtrak, a government-supported passenger rail service, was developed to keep passenger trains rolling in the United States. Amtrak still travels over Marias Pass, and with the growing interest in energy conservation, train travel shows signs of making a comeback.

Streamliners still carry passengers to Glacier National Park. Many people stay just outside the park's boundaries at the Izaak Walton Inn, first built to house railroad workers. In winter the inn is popular with cross-country skiers.

7 Leave No Trace

**The Next Forty Years,
1960–2000**

By the 1960s, nearly 1 million people were visiting Glacier each year. The increasing popularity of the park and advances in scientific research brought many changes to the park over the next forty years. 1967 was a landmark year, when large forest fires and fatal grizzly bear attacks made headlines and caused park managers to rethink how they dealt with fire and wildlife.

BLAZING TRAILS
Changes in Forest Fire Management

In the summer of 1967, several large fires broke out in the park. During this time, people around the nation didn't want to see forests burn, so fires were aggressively fought. Unfortunately this allowed underbrush, fallen trees, and other debris to build up, providing a lot of fuel for any fire that did start. When 1967 rolled around with drier weather, the forest was ready to burn.

However, it was also a time when researchers began to understand that fire isn't always bad. Fire scars on trees showed that fires started by lightning had been a natural part of the area's ecosystem for a very long time. The park's fire regime, meaning the historical pattern of fires' locations, sizes, and severity, shows that typically about fourteen small fires occur each year, with larger fires occurring every few years when the weather is hotter and drier. The fires of 1967 helped lead to changes in the way the Park Service dealt with fire, seeing it as a natural part of Glacier's ecosystem.

Bad fire seasons also occurred in 1988 and 2003, but by then people understood that forest fires can actually help the forest. Fires reduce fuels so future fires don't burn as hot. They change dead plants into ash, which adds nutrients to the soil. Fire also creates openings in the forest where animals can live and feed. Some plants, such as lodgepole pine, quaking aspen, and huckleberry, even grow better after

◀ *Forest fires are a natural part of Glacier's ecosystem. Many plants and animals, including fireweed and three-toed woodpeckers, thrive in habitat created by fire.*

Burned snags from the 1967 Glacier Wall Fire tower above the new forest growing below.
—Donna Love

a forest fire. In time, the open patches become new, young forests, and a forest with trees of varying ages is more resistant to disease.

Today most lightning-caused fires are allowed to burn in certain areas, such as in the backcountry, away from park facilities and people. Fires accidentally started by people, such as by unattended campfires, are almost always fought.

IN THE WOODS
Managing Grizzlies

On August 12, 1967, two campers were killed by different grizzly bears on the same night in two different places in the park. It was a coincidence that the deaths occurred on the same night. In the park's 100-year history, only ten people have died from encounters with the park's bears, including these two instances. That isn't very many, but as you can imagine, two deaths on the same night focused lots of attention on the bears. Some people thought grizzlies should be removed and placed in wilderness areas outside the park. Others thought the bears should stay and that bear management should change—which is what happened in the end.

At the time no one knew how many grizzly bears lived in Glacier, but they did know that a big part of the problem was how food and garbage were handled. Both bears involved in the fatal attacks had been eating regularly at garbage dumps in the park, which was common in national parks at the time. Now we know that when bears get used to eating garbage and human food, they're more likely to be in areas near humans—a situation that's dangerous for

In 1973, grizzly bears in the lower 48 states were placed on the Endangered Species List. Today grizzlies thrive in the park and surrounding areas. —National Park Service

people and bears alike. Strict new rules about food storage and garbage were developed after the attacks to help keep both people and bears safe. Problem bears are removed or killed when necessary.

WARMING TREND
Climate Change and the Park

Throughout the 1970s, park visitation continued to rise. With the new interest in protecting the environment, visitors didn't want to just see Glacier—they wanted to help preserve it, too. As a result, snowmobiles were banned in the park and eventually "Leave No Trace" became the motto for backcountry hiking and camping. Boardwalks were built at popular sites to protect plants, and fishing laws changed to help the park's native fish species thrive.

At the same time it was obvious that the park's glaciers were shrinking. We know now that the glaciers are melting due to climate change, but no one knows for sure whether this change is a natural cycle or caused by humans. What scientists do know is that the earth's climate is getting warmer. In the past 100 years, the average surface temperature of the earth has risen by 1 degree Celsius, which is 1.6 degrees Fahrenheit. That might not seem like a lot, but even minor changes can have a big effect on the earth.

In 1990 Glacier National Park became a part of the U.S. Global Change Research Program, which studies natural and human-caused changes in the environment, and what these changes mean for the future. Higher temperatures in the park could mean longer summers, and that could have big effects on Glacier's plants and animals. The park's water temperature could rise, which would change fish populations. Warmer temperatures especially affect alpine animals, such as mountain goats, snowshoe hares, Canada lynx, marmots, wolverines, ptarmigans, and pikas, which are adapted to a cold, snowy climate. Studies have already begun so the park can tell how these animals are faring.

Animals that turn white in winter for camouflage, like snowshoe hares or this ptarmigan, may have a difficult time with shorter winters and less snowfall.
—National Park Service

As it changes from white winter to brown breeding plumage, this ptarmigan blends in perfectly as spring snow melts. —National Park Service

Snow accumulates in the mountains in winter as snowpack, storing water and slowly releasing it in summer as the snow melts. Less snowpack means less water available in summer. Within the park, this means fewer wetlands and the animals that rely on them, such as ducks and moose. Farther downstream, water shortages could mean changes in food production all across the North American continent. At present, Glacier National Park and the mountains to the south provide 58 percent of Montana's stream flow. That water then flows to other parts of the United States and Canada, so it is very important for all of us to understand the changes that warmer temperatures in the park would bring.

Creatures like the trumpeter swan that depend on glacier's cold, clean water may be among those most affected by climate change. —National Park Service

8 The View Ahead

The Next 100 Years

In the year 2010, Glacier National Park turned 100 years old and annual park visitation soared above the 2 million mark. Despite the growth, the park is finding ways to better serve its many visitors, as well as ways to reduce its own impacts on nature.

SUREFOOTED
Reducing the Park's Carbon Footprint

With concern about climate change growing, the park has been working to reduce its own carbon footprint, which is a measure of the impact human activities have on the environment. One area of concern is greenhouse gases in the atmosphere, which may trap heat in the atmosphere and contribute to climate change.

Carbon dioxide is a major greenhouse gas. Typical motor vehicles produce a lot of carbon dioxide, so transportation is a good place to start reducing carbon footprints. Between 1999 and 2002, Glacier's red jammer buses were restored and retrofitted to run on propane, which releases fewer greenhouse gases. Other park vehicles were converted to use biodiesel, which is produced from renewable resources. You might even see some park employees riding red bicycles. In 2007, to help visitors see more of the park and still reduce the number of cars on the road, Glacier began a free summer shuttle bus service that transports people over Going-to-the-Sun Road.

RISE AND SHINE
Going-to-the-Sun Road in the New Century

Seeing Logan Pass is a wonderful way to learn about alpine habitat. However, Going-to-the-Sun Road celebrated its 75th anniversary in 2008. Years of wear from repeated freezing and thawing, rock and snow avalanches, and the impact of thousands of cars traveling the highway each year mean that a lot of maintenance and construction is needed. Be prepared for road crews and delays, and even closures.

◀ *The park's most famous and regularly seen animals, mountain goats are often used to symbolize the park's pristine mountain ecosystem.*

Clearing snow off Going-to-the-Sun Road is dangerous work that takes up to two months each spring. —National Park Service

Only the lower sections of the road are plowed, so you can't drive over Logan Pass in winter. In spring it takes about two months to clear the road of snow. The park starts clearing the pass in April using bulldozers, rotary blowers, and backhoes. The road is usually cleared of snow and ready to open by mid-June.

The greatest hazard during snow removal is avalanches. An avalanche can bury a bulldozer or send a front-end loader sliding down the mountain. The Big Drift, a snowdrift that forms each winter about a quarter mile east of Logan Pass, is often over 60 feet deep! It's so deep and long that bulldozer drivers sometimes have to guess where the road is.

100 YEARS AND COUNTING
The Park Turns 100

In 2010 Glacier National Park celebrated its one hundredth birthday. The theme of the celebration was "Celebrate, Inspire, Engage." Park officials hoped this theme would motivate people to find ways to become involved with the park.

As Glacier National Park enters its second century, new concerns have emerged. Expanding communities, new homes and businesses, oil and gas exploration, coalmines, rock quarries, goldmines, and roads threaten to surround the park like a hula hoop. If growth continues unchecked Glacier will be cut off from other natural areas outside the park, leaving it an island of wild and scenic beauty surrounded by development.

Without natural corridors animals and plants can't migrate through developed areas, and they won't be able to access habitats they depend on. And without these migration corridors, new animals won't be able to enter the park, resulting in genetic clumping. Genetic clumping happens when living things from the same population continue reproducing with each other over a long period of time. To remain healthy, populations need to have genes from new individuals introduced regularly. Communities, industries, land managers, states, and even countries will need to cooperate to protect enough land outside the park so that wildlife can flourish.

Waterton-Glacier International Peace Park is part of the larger Crown of the Continent ecosystem, which straddles the Continental Divide from Montana to Canada. Keeping natural wildlife migration corridors open is a critical part of keeping wildlife populations healthy in this wild region.

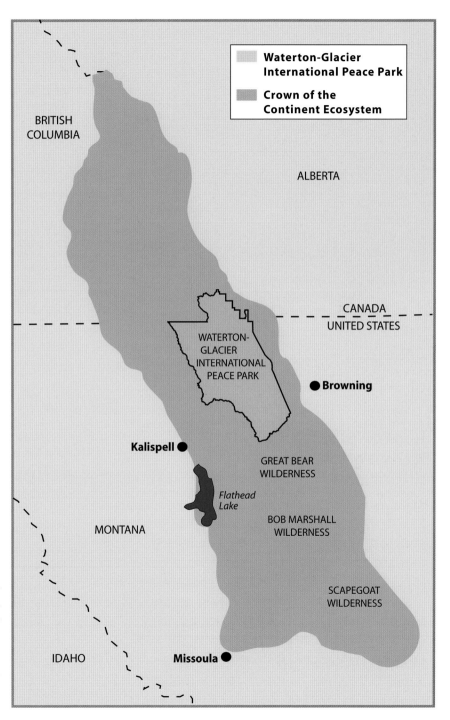

Legend:

- Waterton-Glacier International Peace Park
- **Crown of the Continent Ecosystem**

BRITISH COLUMBIA

ALBERTA

CANADA
UNITED STATES

WATERTON-GLACIER INTERNATIONAL PEACE PARK

● Browning

Kalispell ●

GREAT BEAR WILDERNESS

Flathead Lake

BOB MARSHALL WILDERNESS

MONTANA

SCAPEGOAT WILDERNESS

IDAHO

Missoula ●

RESPONSIBLE RESPECT
The Park's Future and You

In the next century, millions of people from all over the world will visit Glacier National Park. If you are lucky enough to be one of them, you can help the park by becoming an ecotourist. Ecotourists are people who want to minimize their impact on nature and contribute something positive to the places they visit. Before visiting, you could think about ways you can reduce your impact on the park through reducing, reusing, and recycling. To reduce carbon dioxide emissions, ride the free shuttle, which stops at many places, or take a red bus tour. To reuse, refill water bottles instead of buying bottled water. To recycle, use the park's recycle bins. Efforts like these will help the park and the world.

You can also help the park by taking good care of yourself. When surrounded by so much beauty, it is easy to forget that mountain hazards are real. For your own safety, don't go out on glaciers or ice fields, and always cross snow patches carefully. Be careful on rocky high points. That's especially important in Glacier because its sedimentary rock crumbles easily. In addition, be careful around swiftly flowing streams. It may surprise you to learn that the top cause of accidental human death in Glacier is drowning. Always be prepared for changing weather conditions. Even in summer it can snow. If you get chilled and your body's core temperature gets too low (a condition known as hypothermia), it could lead to death.

Never hike alone, and don't jog in the park. You might surprise a bear, or even a mountain lion! Talk or sing loudly,

People from all walks of life can help the park gather important information through the park's Citizen Science Program. Citizen scientists might help count the number of common loon chicks that hatched on the park's lakes or the number of pikas or mountain goats spotted high on a mountainside. —National Park Service

Stay on designated trails or boardwalks to avoid trampling sensitive plants. Also, don't pick the wildflowers. It may have taken ten years for that flower to bloom! —National Park Service

especially at places where you can't see the trail ahead, so the animal knows you're there. Hike in a group and stay close together. Never surround a wild animal or cut off its escape routes. If you are close enough to an animal to change its behavior then you are too close. Be sure to read the park's great information on hiking and camping in wild country and what to do if you encounter a bear or mountain lion.

It's fun to picnic beside a mountain lake or camp below a snowcapped mountain. If you do, be courteous to your human and animal neighbors. Always obey food storage rules, disposing of your garbage properly. Practice "Leave No Trace" rules, and remember: "Pack it in, pack it out." That means that whatever you take in the backcountry with you, you need to bring back out. Never feed the animals— not even the smallest chipmunk. If the animal gets used to eating human food in summer, it may not store enough natural food for winter. And if larger animals like bears get a taste for human food, it can cause problems for both animals and people.

If you see a cool animal, like this black bear, on a road, let the animal pass safely, then drive on slowly. If you stop to look at it, and others stop, too, it may cause a "bear jam," which could cause the animal or people to get hurt.
—National Park Service

Most importantly, the land in Glacier National Park is still mostly in its natural state. Its plants and animals need this wild, undisturbed habitat to survive. We're making progress on understanding and protecting the park. We've learned how to allow natural fires to play their role in the ecosystem and how to live alongside the grizzly. We need to continue to work together to help limit human impacts and development that might harm the park. By studying its shrinking glaciers, we can learn how to protect the park's plants and animals in the future—and how to help the broader ecosystem, our nation, and our planet.

To learn more about Glacier, you can stop by its visitor centers at Apgar, Logan Pass, or St. Mary, where you can become a Junior Ranger and participate in fun educational activities that will help you learn more about the park. Even if you can't visit the park, you can become a WebRanger online!
—National Park Service

Glacier National Park truly is the crown of our continent, and it deserves the care of all people so it can endure, vibrant and intact, forever. —National Park Service

TOTALLY FUN FACTS

➤ Today's glaciers are still carving Glacier National Park, but they only move one to two inches a week, so it would take many years before you would notice a change.

➤ Like water, ice absorbs light from the red end of the spectrum and reflects blue, so ice in a glacier may appear blue. The deeper the blue, the older the ice probably is.

➤ Running Eagle Falls was named for Running Eagle, Pita Omarkan or Pitamakan, a legendary Blackfeet woman warrior who visited the falls on spiritual quests.

➤ Glacier's streams are so important to the nation's water supply that they are sometimes called the "headwaters of the continent."

➤ Even though the water in Glacier National Park appears pure, visitors should never drink directly from a lake or stream. The giardia parasite, which can make people very sick, may be in some of the lakes and streams. Hikers and campers should use a water purification system.

➤ Native people weave watertight baskets from the grass-like leaves of beargrass, leading to another of its common names, Indian basket grass. Beargrass thrives after fires, sprouting from rhizomes (kind of like bulbs) underground.

➤ Unlike deer and elk, which shed their antlers and regrow them each year, the mountain goat doesn't lose its horns. Each year a mountain goat's horns grow larger. These horns grow up to 12 inches long on both the male and female, but a nanny's horns are slimmer than a billy's. Female and male mountain goats are only together in fall, so if you see several mountain goats together in summer they are probably all nannies and a few young, or a few billies hanging out together.

➤ One of Glacier's most enduring legends is a "fishy story" about the water being so cold that fish had to grow fur to survive. It seems that in the early 1900s a group of anglers had a coat of fur put on a trout in a local taxidermy shop. Pictures of the fur-bearing trout circulated in hundreds of newspapers throughout the United States. To advertise the park, the Great Northern Railway had the picture put on postcards. The fur-bearing fish postcard was a favorite park souvenir for many years.

➤ The Kootenai held ceremonies on the banks of Lake McDonald, so they called it *Yakil Hagwilnamki*, which means, "a good place to dance." It earned its current name from Duncan McDonald, a fur freighter, who carved his name on a birch tree by the lake in 1878 while on a cargo delivery to Canada.

➤ Granite Park Chalet is misnamed. There is no granite in the park. However, the Purcell Sill is made of a dark rock called diorite that is sometimes called black granite.

➤ Two Medicine Lake was named for two medicine lodges, or ceremonial lodges, that the Blood and Piegan tribes of the Blackfeet set up on opposite sides of the lake.

➤ In 1933 when Going-to-the-Sun Road was completed, a dedi-cation ceremony was held at the top of the pass. Only 2,000 people were expected for the ceremony, but 4,000 showed up, so the park served smaller portions of the hot dog and chili lunch to feed everyone.

➤ On average, 400 people hike to Hidden Lake on Logan Pass every hour during the summer months. Now you know why everyone needs to obey park rules and stay on the boardwalk and trail! With that many people, the wildflowers wouldn't have a chance to grow otherwise.

SELECTED GLOSSARY

alpine. Describes the habitat or climate high in the mountains above tree line, where summers are short and winters are long.

arête. Long, thin ridge formed when two glaciers scrape against opposite sides of a mountain.

cirque. Bowl-shaped mountainside left behind by a glacier.

climate. The average weather conditions in a particular region over a long period of time.

climate change. Natural or human-caused changes in climate over a period of decades or longer.

col. A low place on a mountain ridge; also called a saddle or pass.

crevasse. A deep crack in a glacier or ice sheet.

ecosystem. A particular environment and the community of plants and animals that live there.

elevation. How high above sea level something is.

fault. Fracture or break in a rock formation.

fire regime. The pattern of fire occurrence, size, and severity in a given area.

glacial till. Rocks and other debris moved and deposited by a glacier.

glacier. A large mass of moving ice that remains from year to year.

habitat. The natural environment of a plant or animal.

hanging valley. A small valley that "hangs" above a larger valley below.

headwaters. Where a stream or river begins to flow.

horn. Pyramid-shaped mountain shaped by the action of three or more glaciers.

ice age. A cold period marked by episodes of glaciation.

krummholz. German for "crooked wood." Describes vegetation at tree line that has been stunted and deformed by wind and cold.

limestone. A sedimentary rock often formed from an accumulation of calcite and other remains of marine life.

magma. Hot liquid rock beneath the surface of the earth; called lava when it emerges through a volcano.

meltwater. Water melted from snow or ice, including glacial ice; meltwater provides a water supply in many places.

migration. The natural movements of animals as they travel, usually seasonally, between feeding, breeding, and wintering ranges.

moraine. A ridgelike accumulation of rocks and dirt deposited at the edge of a glacier.

Pleistocene. The epoch that began 2.5 million years ago and ended about 12,000 years ago. It included the Ice Age, the last major period of glaciation.

sediment. Particles of natural materials, such as rocks and organic matter, that have been broken down and transported by the actions of wind, water, and ice.

sedimentary rock. Rock formed from the deposit of sediment.

subalpine. Describes the mountain habitat at tree line, just below the alpine zone.

tarn. A mountain lake in a cirque.

tree line. The area on a mountain where the alpine zone begins. Above the tree line trees can't grow due to cold and wind.

weather. The temperature, wind, and precipitation (rain or snow) at a particular time and place.

weathering. The breaking down and wearing away of rock by the actions of water, wind, and ice.

GET TOTALLY OUT THERE AND EXPLORE SOME MORE

WEBSITES

Crown of the Continent Ecosystem
www.crownofthecontinent.org

Glacier Association
www.glacierassociation.org

Glacier Institute
www.glacierinstitute.org

Glacier National Park Citizen Science Program
http://home.nps.gov/glac/naturescience/
ccrlc-citizen-science.htm

Glacier National Park Fund
www.glacierfund.org

Glacier National Park Official Web Site
 www.nps.gov/glac

Glacier National Park Webcams
www.nps.gov/glac/photosmultimedia/webcams.htm

**USGS Repeat Photography Project,
Glacier National Park, Montana**
http://www.nrmsc.usgs.gov/repeatphoto/overview.htm

BOOKS FOR KIDS

Glacier National Park. John Hamilton. Edina, Minn.: ABDO
Publishing, 2005.
*Explore the history of the park with this photographer/writer.
Includes topographic map.*

Glacier National Park. Mike Graf. Mankato, Minn.: Bridgestone
Books, 2004.
*Even young readers can learn about Glacier National Park in this
short, to-the-point book filled with beautiful photographs and a
map activity.*

Glacier National Park: An ABC Adventure. KC Glastetter and Jeremie
Hollman. Missoula, Mont.: Mountain Press Publishing, 2008.
*Join nature photographers KC Glastetter and Jeremie Hollman on
a letter-by-letter journey through the Crown of the Continent.*

*Glacier National Park Legends and Lore: Along Going-to-the-Sun
Road*. C. W. Guthrie. Helena, Mont.: Farcountry Press, 2002.
*Journey over Logan Pass with mountain man Hugh Monroe, who
recounts legends and history of American Indians and early settlers
encountered along the way.*

OTHER BOOKS

Glacier National Park: The First 100 Years. C. W. Guthrie. Helena,
Mont.: Farcountry Press, 2008.

*Hiking Glacier and Waterton Lakes National Parks: A Guide to More
Than 60 of the Area's Greatest Hiking Adventures*. Erik Molvar.
Guilford, Conn: Falcon, 2007.

It Happened in Glacier National Park. Vince Moravek. Guilford,
Conn.: TwoDot Books, 2005.

Logan Pass: Alpine Splendor in Glacier National Park. Jerry DeSanto.
Helena, Mont.: Falcon Press, 1995.

Wildflowers of Glacier National Park and Surrounding Areas.
Shannon Fitzpatrick Kimball and Peter Lesica. Missoula, Mont.:
Mountain Press, 2010.

INDEX

Page numbers with illustrations appear in **boldface**.

A. J. LOVE

ABOUT THE AUTHOR

Artist and award-winning author **Donna Love** has written numerous nature books for young people. She regularly brings her interactive natural history and art programs to grade schools and public events in Montana and the Pacific Northwest. She feels that the more she can help people learn about an animal or place, the more likely they'll be to help care for it. This is Donna's third book with illustrator Joyce Turley for Mountain Press, following *Loons: Diving Birds of the North* and *Awesome Ospreys: Fishing Birds of the World*. To see more of her work go to donnalove.com.

Donna makes her home in Seeley Lake, Montana, where her husband, Tim, is the district ranger for the U.S. Forest Service. They have three grown children and one granddaughter.

RICHARD T. TURLEY

ABOUT THE ILLUSTRATOR

Joyce Mihran Turley specializes in presenting images of nature to readers of all ages. Many of her award-winning books focus on introducing children to native animals and unique ecosystems, including such national parks as Everglades, Grand Canyon, and Yellowstone. With a background in applied mathematics and engineering as well as fine art, she has a technical perspective that results in vibrant illustrations with a unique balance of analytic and artistic elements. Joyce's online gallery is available at dixoncovedesign.com.

Raised in upstate New York, Joyce has lived with her husband in the foothills of the Colorado Rockies for over thirty years. Her studio, located in their now-empty nest, permits convenient observation of deer, coyotes, lizards, eagles, and snakes—just outside the picture windows!